Preface

This book is for church choirs of all types and sizes wh〔
All the anthems in this book can be performed by a mi
ible arrangements also enable them to be performed by a wide variety of other
groups, including upper-voice choirs, choirs with few men, unison choirs, small
choirs, and choirs just starting out. The book thus meets a very real need of
church choirs today in offering flexibility of scoring in a constructive and real-
istic way.

The collection presents a wide variety of repertoire for all types of occasion.
There are flexible arrangements of favourite anthems alongside less familiar
pieces. There are new arrangements of plainsong melodies and of folk
tunes from several continents. In addition, a number of anthems have been
specially commissioned, enabling a wide range of musical styles to be repre-
sented. The emphasis throughout is on practicality and accessibility, without
ever compromising on musical integrity and quality.

Vocal scoring

All the possible scorings for each anthem are shown in a box at the top of the
first page of each piece. The basic principle is that anything in brackets may be
omitted. Additionally, parts simply marked **VOICE** can be sung by upper voices,
or men, or a combination of both.

Here are examples of the principal scorings used:

S A (T) B Keyboard	This may be performed with four vocal parts and keyboard, or the tenor part may be omitted, with all men singing the bass part.
S A (Men) Keyboard	There is a unison men's part, suitable for tenors and basses, which may be omitted to make an upper-voice anthem with keyboard.
S (A) (Men) Keyboard	This may be sung as a unison anthem with all voices singing the soprano/melody line (men an octave lower), or by upper voices in two parts, or in three parts for S A Men, all with keyboard accompaniment. Alternatively, the alto part may be omitted to create a two-part anthem for upper voices, men's voices, and keyboard.
S (A) (T) (B) (Keyboard)*	This can be sung by SATB *a cappella*, or by unison voices (singing the soprano/melody line) or any vocal combination including soprano, with keyboard accompaniment. * The keyboard part may be omitted when all voice parts are present, or as indicated by the footnote.

Voices 1 2
Keyboard

This may be sung by any combination of voices in two parts, for example Voice 1 (Soprano and/or Tenor) and Voice 2 (Alto and/or Bass), or by Voice 1 (upper voices) and Voice 2 (men), all with keyboard accompaniment. More specific suggestions are sometimes given during the course of the anthem.

Voices 1 (2) (3)
Keyboard

This may be sung in unison or in two or three parts with any appropriate combination of voices, either upper, men, or mixed.

Further clarification on scoring is given in a footnote where necessary.

In some anthems there is a DESCANT towards the end. This is optional, and may in most cases be sung by sopranos and/or tenors, either full or as a semi-chorus.

Occasionally, individual voice parts will divide, with two notes indicated on the same stem. If both notes are large, then either or both may be sung. If one note is small, then the larger is preferable, but the smaller is an acceptable alternative (or again, both may be sung).

Where there are passages in unison, vocal options are usually specified, but others may be substituted if preferred. Using contrasting groups—upper and lower voices, solo and tutti—will help give variety to the different verses or sections.

In short, choir leaders may choose from the many different scoring options available to make the most appropriate use of the singers at their disposal and perform the anthems in the way which suits them best.

An Appendix listing the original versions and scorings of those anthems where more substantial arrangements or adaptations have been made for the purposes of this book is given on p. 284.

Keyboard parts

In almost every case the keyboard parts have been arranged to be suitable for playing on an organ with pedals, or organ manuals only, or piano. Players may wish to exercise their judgement in some instances, bearing the following guidelines in mind:

Organ with pedals: Play everything you can, following the bracketed **Man.** and **Ped.** markings. Ignore the occasional markings for the piano sustaining pedal and any piano notes which go out of range. The left-hand part is frequently shared between the staves, and cross-staff lines clarify this where necessary.

Organ manuals only: ignore the bracketed **Man.** and **Ped.** markings and any solo stops that are not practicable, and omit any small notes that cannot be reached.

THE OXFORD BOOK OF
Flexible Anthems

A COMPLETE RESOURCE FOR
EVERY CHURCH CHOIR

EDITED BY ALAN BULLARD

MUSIC DEPARTMENT

OXFORD
UNIVERSITY PRESS

OXFORD
UNIVERSITY PRESS

Great Clarendon Street, Oxford OX2 6DP, England
198 Madison Avenue, New York, NY 10016, USA

Oxford University Press is a department of the University of Oxford.
It furthers the University's aim of excellence in research, scholarship,
and education by publishing worldwide

Oxford is a registered trade mark of Oxford University Press
in the UK and in certain other countries

Database right Oxford University Press (maker)

First published 2007

5 7 9 10 8 6

ISBN 978-0-19-335895-9 (paperback)
ISBN 978-0-19-335896-6 (wiro)

Music origination by
Barnes Music Engraving Ltd., East Sussex
Printed in Great Britain on acid-free paper by
Caligraving Ltd., Thetford, Norfolk

Piano: Ignore the organ-specific instructions and omit any small notes that cannot be reached. Adapt the music for piano by repeating long pedal notes that would be sustained on the organ, or doubling the bass line in octaves, or using the sustaining pedal where appropriate.

It is worth noting that although the accompaniments may be played on piano or organ, some are more suitable for one instrument than the other. If you are lucky enough to have both instruments available, choose the one which suits the anthem best.

In several anthems there are sections where the keyboard part is entirely in small notes, or where doubling 'ad lib.' is indicated. If desired, the keyboard can be omitted if all voices are present, but it should normally be played if they are not. Above all, remember that the keyboard part is designed to support the choir, adding musical interest but not detracting from the singing or the projection of the words.

Words, tempi, and expression

The starting point for every anthem is the words—they set the speed, mood, style, expression, and character of the anthem. Metronome marks are provided, but these are only suggestions, as the optimum tempo will vary according to the circumstances and the size and acoustic of the building in which the anthem is performed. Clarity of words is essential, and this should also guide the choice of tempo. A slight emphasis on the important words will help to shape the phrases musically. When learning a new anthem, focus right from the beginning on the sense of the words, as well as the notes and rhythms. This will help choirs to develop a deeper understanding of the anthem and its meaning.

The intention of this collection is to enable all choirs, of whatever size or composition, to sing to the glory of God every Sunday and on each principal feast day of the year (with the exception of Christmas, for which there are many carol and other collections available). I hope it meets that expectation and that choirs will find it an invaluable aid to worship.

I would like to thank all those who have given helpful advice and made suggestions of anthems or texts to include, in particular Julian Elloway and Helen Burrows, and the editorial team at OUP for all their help and care with this project.

Alan Bullard
Summer 2007

Index of Titles and First Lines

Where first lines differ from titles, the former are shown in italics.

Listing by Liturgical Year and Themes
with Scoring

Many anthems are also suitable for general use.
For further details on scoring, see Preface.

TITLE	SCORING	COMPOSER/ARRANGER	PAG
Advent			
Christ is the world's true Light	Voices 1 (2) Kbd	Stanton	3
Creator of the stars of night	S (A) (Men) Kbd	arr. Scott	5
Gabriel to Mary came	S (A) (T) (B) (Kbd)	arr. Bullard	7
(Angelus ad virginem)			
Hark, the glad sound!	S (A) (Men) Kbd	Thorne	9
Jesus Christ the Apple Tree	S (A) (Men) Kbd	arr. Bullard	13
Let all mortal flesh keep silence	Voices 1 (2) Kbd	arr. Cleobury	14
Magnificat	S (A) (Men) Kbd	Shera	6
Never weather-beaten sail	S (A) (Men) Kbd	Campion, adap. Bullard	16
There is no rose	Voices 1 (2) Kbd	Smith	25
Epiphany			
Brightest and best of the sons	S (A) (Men) Kbd	Archer	1
of the morning			
Christ is the world's true Light	Voices 1 (2) Kbd	Stanton	3
Star of Wonder	S (A) (Men) Kbd	Bullard	22
Presentation of Christ in the Temple			
Christ is the world's true Light	Voices 1 (2) Kbd	Stanton	3
Nunc dimittis	Voices 1 (2) Kbd	Shera	6
Lent			
A Prayer of St Richard of Chichester	S S (A) (T) (B) Kbd	White, adap. Bullard	19
Bread of the world	S (A) (T) (B) Kbd	arr. Bullard	1
Hide not thou thy face	S (A) (Men) or	Farrant	11
	SATB (Kbd)		
Lamb of God (Agnus Dei)	Voices 1 (2) Kbd	Webbe	14
O for a closer walk with God	S A (T) (B) Kbd	Stanford	17
O God of mercy	Voices 1 (2) Kbd	Lole	17
Passiontide			
Drop, drop, slow tears	Voices 1 2 (Men) Kbd	Andrew	5
God so loved the world	S A (T) (B) Kbd	Bullard	8
Hosanna to the Son of David	S (A) (Men) Kbd	Telemann	12
Jesu, Lamb of God, Redeemer	S A (Men) Kbd	Elgar	13
(Ave verum corpus)			
Were you there?	Voices 1 (2) (3) Kbd	arr. Hunt	26
Where all charity and love are	Voices 1 2 Kbd	arr. Bullard	27
(Ubi caritas)			
Wondrous Cross	S A (Men) Kbd	Wilby	27

1. Alleluia

WILLIAM BOYCE (1711–79)
accomp. Alan Bullard

* The keyboard part may be omitted if all three voice parts are sung; begin at either bar 5 or bar 21.

S A (T) (B)
Keyboard

2. Author of life divine

Charles Wesley
(1707–88)

CECILIA McDOWALL
(b. 1951)

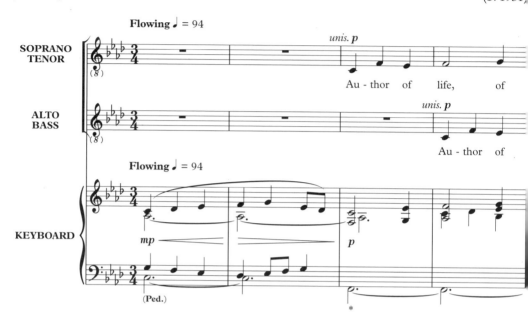

* If performing on piano, repeat the tied bass notes as required throughout.

S (A) (Men)
Keyboard

3. Be still, for the presence of the Lord

Words and music by
DAVID J. EVANS (b. 1957)
arr. Richard Shephard

If performing in unison, sing the melody throughout, omitting the descant sections in vv. 2 and 3.

S (A) (T) (B)
Keyboard

4. Bread of the world

Reginald Heber
(1783–1826)

Trad. Scottish
arr. ALAN BULLARD (b. 1947)

This anthem may be shortened by omitting bars 22–41.

optional cut to bar 42

death_ our sins___ are dead._____

(Man.)

S./A. *unis.* or SOLO *p legato*

Look on the heart_ by sor - row bro - ken, Look on the

tears_ by sin - ners shed;___ And be your feast___ to us___ the

to - ken That by your grace_ our souls___ are fed._____

for Phillip Bell and the boys of Eccles Hall School, Norfolk

S (A) (Men)
Keyboard

5. Brightest and best of the sons of the morning

Reginald Heber
(1783–1826)

MALCOLM ARCHER
(b. 1952)

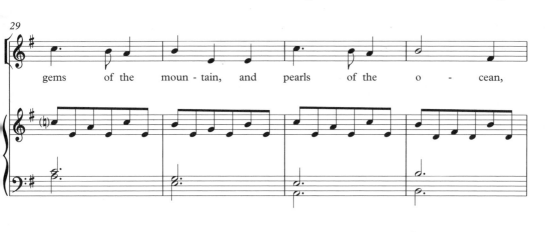

gems   of the   moun - tain,   and   pearls   of the   o -   cean,

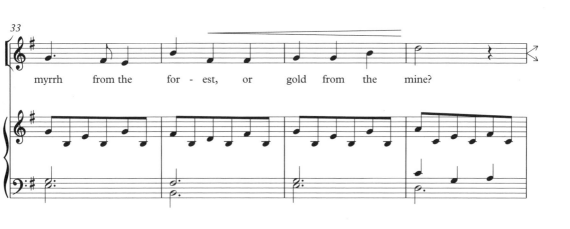

myrrh   from the   for - est,   or   gold   from   the   mine?

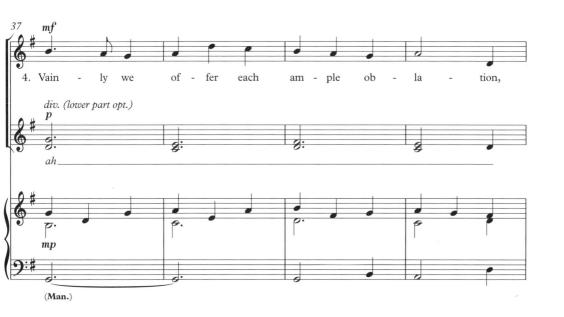

4. Vain - ly   we   of - fer   each   am - ple   ob - la - tion,

div. (lower part opt.)

ah

(**Man.**)

vain - ly   with   gifts would his   fa - vour   se - cure: rich - er   by

ah

far   is   the   heart's a - do - ra - tion,   dear - er   to   God are   the

ah

prayers   of the   poor.

(Ped.)

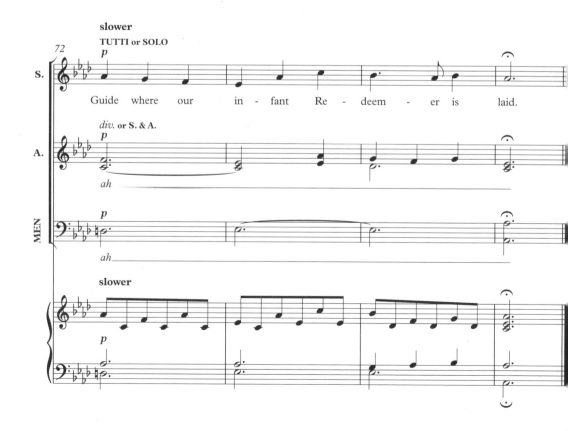

S (A) (T) (B)
Keyboard

6. Christians, shout for joy and gladness

trans. C. S. Philips

Melody and figured bass by J. S. BACH (1685–1750)
additional parts by Alan Bullard

Hell's_ dark pow - ers flee___ be - fore___ him; Christ - ians,
unis.

has - ten to_____ a - dore him. Sa - tan can - not

harm_ you now:_____ Sin's_____ do - min - ion is_____ laid_

* Keyboard: double voice parts *ad lib.*

Voices 1 (2)
Keyboard

7. Christ is the world's true Light

George Wallace Briggs
(1875–1959)

WALTER KENDALL STANTON
(1891–1978)

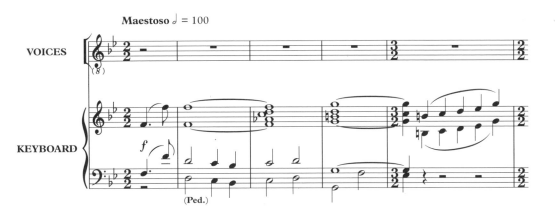

their an-cient feuds for-get-ting, The whole round world com-plete, from sun-rise to its set-ting. When Christ is throned as Lord, we shall for-sake our fear; To plough-share beat the sword, to prun-ing hook the spear.

cresc.

S (A) (Men)
Keyboard

8. Christ the Lord is ris'n again!

Michael Weisse (*c.*1480–*c.*1530)
trans. Catherine Winkworth

RICHARD SHEPHARD
(b. 1949)

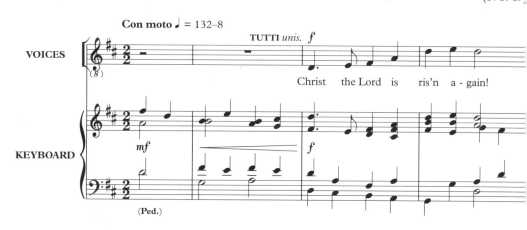

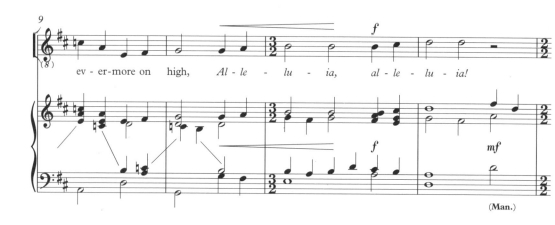

He who gave for us his life,___ Who for us en -

- dured the strife,___ Is our Pas-chal Lamb to - day! We too sing for joy and

say Al - le - lu - ia, al - le - lu - ia!

(Ped.)

52

poco rit.

ff

f

a tempo

55

TUTTI *unis.*

f

Thou,   our Pas - chal Lamb in - deed,   Christ, to-day your   peo - ple feed;

59

DESCANT   f

Take   our   sins and guilt   a - way,   Let   us   sing   by night and

OTHER VOICES

rit.

*Al - le - lu - ia,_____   ff

63

S.

A.

day,   *Al - le - lu - ia,   al - le - lu - ia!_____

*Al - le - lu - ia,_____

MEN *div.*

*Al - le - lu - ia,   ff

*Al - le - lu - ia,

rit.

ff

ff

* If performing in unison, sing the upper men's part from bar 63 to the end.

for Clare College, Cambridge

9. A Clare Benediction

S A Men
(or Unis.)
Piano*

Words and music by
JOHN RUTTER (b. 1945)

* The original version of the accompaniment, for organ, is compatible with the voice parts of this arrangement, and is found in the SATB version of the anthem (978–0–19–351152–1).

* If performing in unison, sing the men's part from bar 56 (beat 3) to bar 64 (beat 2).

for Tim and Nat

S A (T) (B)*
Keyboard

10. Come down, O Love divine

Bianco da Siena (d. 1434)
trans. R. F. Littledale

HILARY TADMAN-ROBINS
(b. 1947)

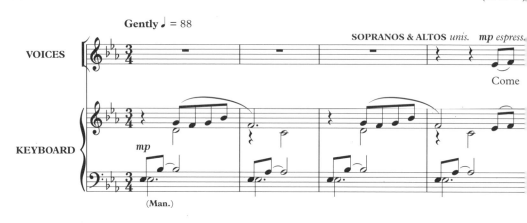

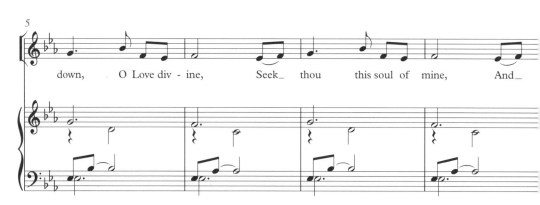

* Sing tenor rather than bass if few men are available.

to Jeremy S. Bruns and the Choir of St Paul's Cathedral, Buffalo, NY

S (A) (Men) Keyboard

11. Creator of the stars of night

7th-cent. Office Hymn
trans. J. M. Neale (altd.)

Mode iv melody
arr. JOHN SCOTT (b. 1956)

Cre - a - tor of the stars of night, Thy peo-ple's ev - er-last-ing light, O Je - su, Sa-viour of us all, Re - gard thy ser-vants when they

13

(8) call.

MEN or ALTOS *mf*

Thou, grie-ving at the bit-ter

cresc.

mf

18

(8) cry   Of   all cre - a - tion doomed to   die,   Didst   come to save a ruin-ed

22

(8) race   With   heal-ing gifts of heav'n-ly grace.

cresc.

27

unis. mf

Thou cam-est, bride-groom of the   bride,   As

mf

f   *mf*

drew the world to even-ing - tide, Pro - ceed-ing from a vir - gin shrine, The

Son of Man, yet Lord di - vine.

TUTTI *unis.* *f*

At thy great name, ma-jes-tic

cresc.

now, All knees must bend, all hearts must bow, And things in heav'n and earth shall

Voices 1 2
(Men)*
Keyboard

12. Drop, drop, slow tears

Phineas Fletcher
(1582–1650)

KERRY ANDREW
(b. 1978)

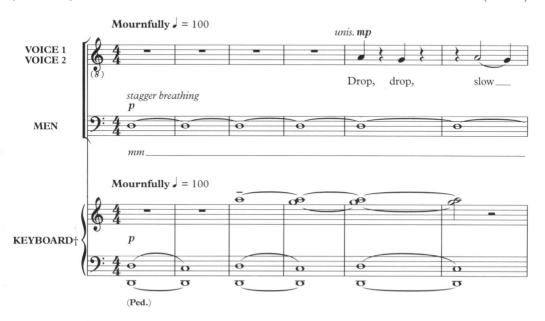

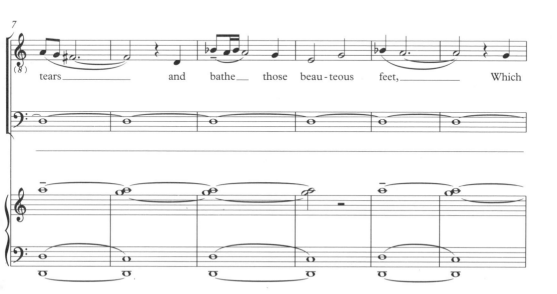

* Voices 1 and 2 may be sung by upper voices or men, but the optional third part must be sung by men only.
† If playing the accompaniment on piano, use the sustaining pedal *ad lib.* to create a wash of sound throughout.

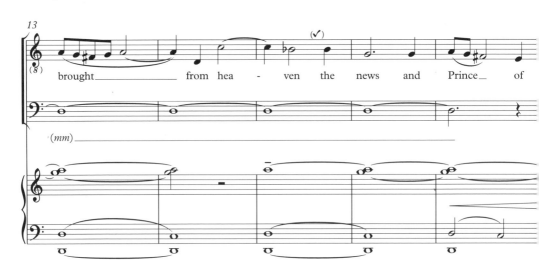

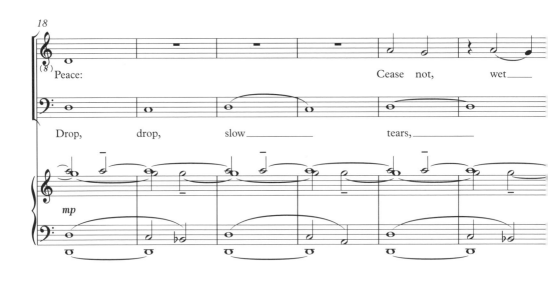

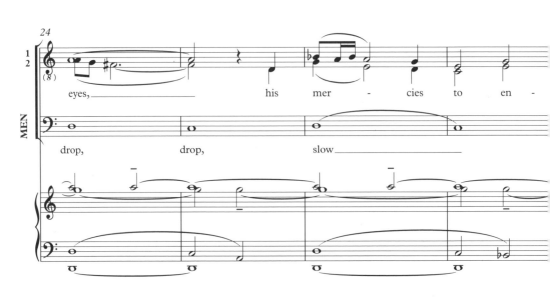

(**Organ**: sustain ped. D until the end)

S (A) (Men)
Keyboard

13. Evening Service in C
Magnificat

FRANK HENRY SHERA
(1882–1956)

Voices 1 (2)
Keyboard

Nunc dimittis

FRANK HENRY SHERA
(1882–1956)

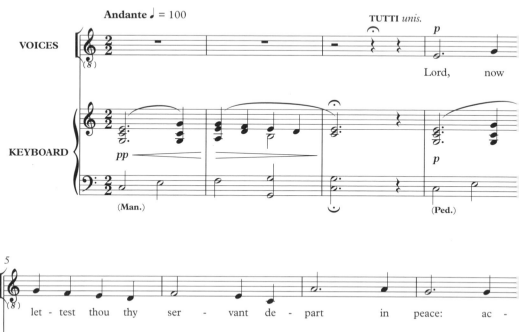

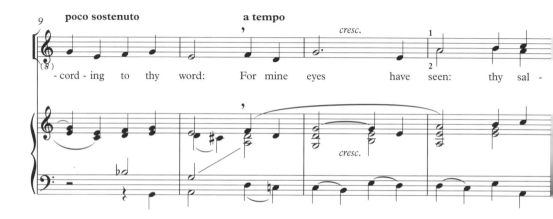

S (A) (Men)
Keyboard

14. Fairest Lord Jesus

17th-cent. German
trans. Lilian Sinclair Stevenson

Silesian folk song (1842)
arr. MARTIN HOW (b. 1931)

* Keyboard: double voice parts *ad lib.*

15. Gabriel to Mary came
(Angelus ad virginem)

Arundel MS (13th cent.)
trans. W. A. C. Pickard-Cambridge (adap.)

Melody: 14th-cent. Irish
arr. Alan Bullard (b. 1947)

(Man. v. 1; Ped. v. 4)

* This piece may be performed in two parts (with scoring as marked) with or without keyboard, or in unison with keyboard. If performing unaccompanied, omit the introduction and the empty bars between the verses. Simple percussion may be added if desired.

* v. 2: if there are insufficient singers to make the suggested contrast between SA and TB effective, use fewer singers in bars 29–36 and sing tutti thereafter.

Repeat for v. 3, then
D.S. *v. 4 to* **Fine**

* If performing with unison voices, sing lower part only from bar 41 (beat 2) to bar 50.

S (A) (Men)
(Keyboard)*

16. Give thanks to God

Alan Bullard

Trad. Botswanan
arr. ALAN BULLARD (b. 1947)

* This anthem may be performed in unison (sing from the upper stave) with keyboard, or in three parts (sing from the lower staves) with or without keyboard.

S (A) (Men)
(Keyboard)

17. God be in my head

From a Book of Hours
(Sarum, 1514)

CECIL ARMSTRONG GIBBS
(1889–1960)

God be in my mouth, And in my speak - ing;__ God be in my heart, And in my

think - ing;__ God be at mine end, And at my de - part - ing.

end, And at my de - part - ing.

S A (Men)
Keyboard

18. God in Mine Eternity

Trad. Hebridean

ALAN BULLARD
(b. 1947)

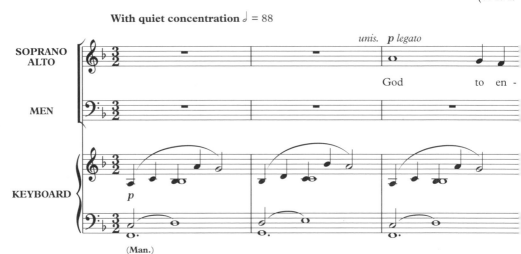

S A (T) (B)
Keyboard

19. God so loved the world

John 3: 16–17

ALAN BULLARD
(b. 1947)

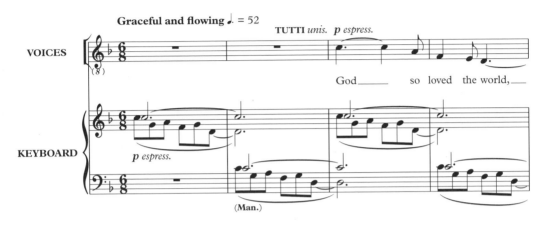

all who be-lieve__ in him shall not pe-rish,_____ but have ev-er-

all who be-lieve in him_____ shall not pe-rish but have ev-er-

-last-ing life,_____ ev-er-last-ing life,_____ ev-er-last - ing_____

-last - ing life,_____ ev-er-last - ing, ev - er - last - ing_____

-last - ing life,_____ ev - er - last - ing_____

in memory of my father

S (A) (Men)
Keyboard

20. God that madest earth and heaven

v. 1: Reginald Heber (1783–1826)
v. 2: Richard Whatley (1787–1863)

Trad. Welsh
arr. DAVID THORNE (b. 1950)

For____ rest the night. May thine_ an - gel guards de - fend_ us, Slum - ber_ sweet thy mer - cy send us,__ Ho - ly dreams and hopes at-tend us This_ live - long night.

(**Organ: Solo Flute**)

* Lower part optional

S (A) (T) (B)*
(Keyboard)†

21. Hail, Virgin Mary
(Ave Maria)

The Angelic Salutation

FRANZ LISZT
(1811–86)

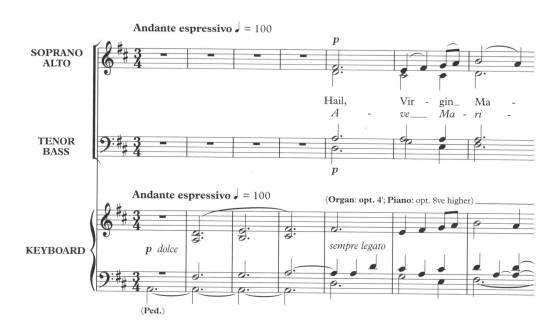

* Sing bass rather than tenor if few men are available.

† The keyboard part (and the introduction) may be omitted if all four voice parts are sung.

to David Hopgood and the Choir of St John's Cathedral, Portsmouth

S (A) (Men)
Keyboard

22. Hark, the glad sound!

Philip Doddridge
(1702–51)

DAVID THORNE
(b. 1950)

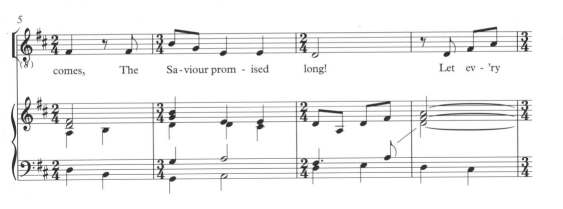

* If performing in unison, sing the alto part from bar 65 to the end.

SATB (T) B
(Keyboard)*

23. Harvest Carol

J. S. B. Monsell
(1811–75)

IAN RAY
(b. 1946)

Joyous and with movement ♪ = 200
(*Always follow the natural accentuation of the words*)

VOICES
(KEYBOARD
tacet

S./A. 1. Sing to the Lord of har - vest, Sing songs of love and praise;
T./B. 2. By him the clouds drop fat - ness, The de-serts bloom and spring,
S./A. 3. Heap on his sa - cred al - tar The gifts his good-ness gave,

With joy - ful hearts and voi - ces Your al - le - lu - ias raise:
The hills leap up in glad - ness, The val - leys laugh and sing;
The gold - en sheaves of har - vest, The souls he died to save:

v. 3 to Coda ⊕

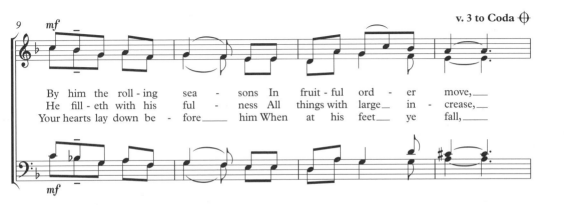

By him the roll - ing sea - sons In fruit - ful ord - er move,
He fill - eth with his ful - ness All things with large in - crease,
Your hearts lay down be - fore him When at his feet ye fall,

* This anthem may be sung *a cappella* in three or four parts, or with keyboard accompaniment as marked.

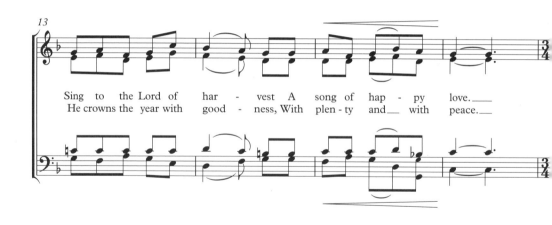

Sing to the Lord of har - vest A song of hap - py love.___
He crowns the year with good - ness, With plen - ty and___ with peace.___

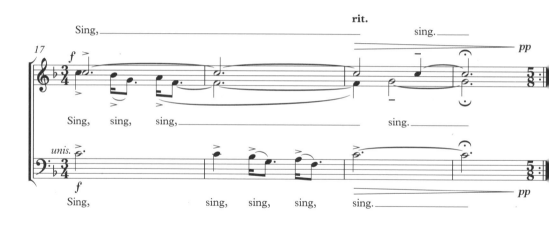

Sing,___ sing.___
Sing, sing, sing,___ sing.___
Sing, sing, sing, sing, sing.___

And with your lives a - dore___ him, Who gave his life___ for all.___

to William Lovelock

Voices 1 2
Keyboard

24. He is risen

Mrs C. F. Alexander
(1823–95)

CECIL COPE

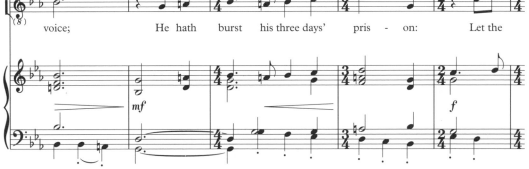

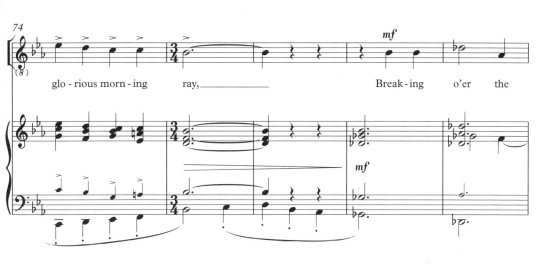

glo - rious morn - ing ray,_____ Break - ing o'er the

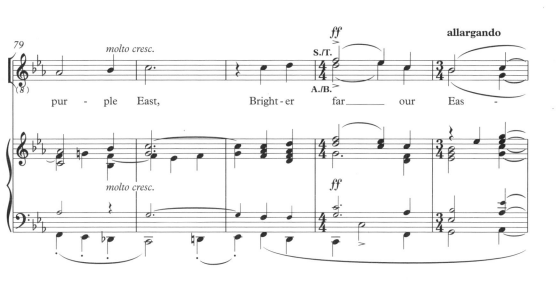

pur - ple East, Bright - er far our Eas -

- ter feast._____

S (A) (Men)
or S A T B
(Keyboard)*

25. Hide not thou thy face

Psalm 27: 10

RICHARD FARRANT
(d. 1580)

* This piece may be sung *a cappella* in three parts (sing from the upper staves) or four parts (sing from the lower staves). It may also be sung in two parts or in unison (sing from the upper staves), using the lower staves as a keyboard accompaniment. The SATB version is Farrant's original.

26. Holy, holy, holy, Holy is the Lord

FRANZ SCHUBERT (1797–1828)
accomp. Alan Bullard

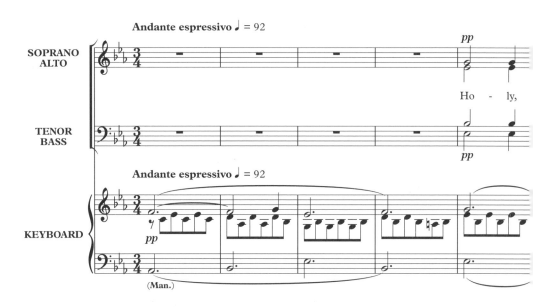

* The keyboard part may be omitted when all four voice parts are sung. This *a cappella* version is Schubert's original.

S (A) Men
Keyboard

27. Holy, holy, holy! Lord God Almighty!

Reginald Heber
(1783–1826)

ALAN SMITH
(b. 1962)

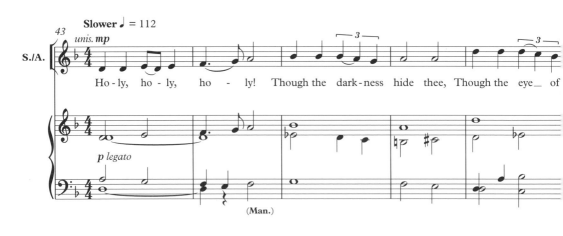

S (A) (Men)
Keyboard

28. Hosanna to the Son of David

Matthew 21: 9

GEORG PHILIPP TELEMANN
(1681–1767)

Cut from bar 24 (beat 2) to bar 49 (beat 1) to form a short introit.

- san - na,   sing ho - san - na,   to the Son of Da - vid,   sing ho

Sing ho-san - na,   to the Son_____ of Da - vid, sing ho-san - na,

Sing ho-san - na,   to the Son of Da - vid, sing ho-san - na,

- san-na,   sing ho - san-na,   to the Son of Da - vid, the Son of Da -

sing ho-san-na,   to the Son_____ of Da - vid, the Son of Da -

sing ho-san-na,   to the Son of Da - vid, the Son of Da -

* Only sing small notes if cut is made.

Lord, in the name of the Lord, Sing ho-san-na in the high-est, in the high-est, in the

high - est, Sing ho-san-na in the high-est, in the high-est, in the

Lord,__ of the Lord, Sing ho-san-na in the high-est, in the high-est, in the

molto rall.

high - est, sing ho - san-na in the high-est, sing ho - san-na in the high - est!

high - est, sing ho - san-na in the high-est, sing ho - san-na in the high - est!

high - est, sing ho - san-na in the high-est, sing ho - san-na in the high - est!

molto rall.

for Grupo Vocal Olisipo

29. Irish Blessing

S (A) (Men)
Keyboard

Trad.

BOB CHILCOTT
(b. 1955)

road rise to meet you,___ may the wind be ev-er at your back, may the

sun shine warm up - on___ your face, and the rain fall soft up-on your fields,___

wind be ev-er at your back, may the sun shine warm up-on_ your face, and the

rain fall soft up-on your fields,_____

rain fall soft up-on your fields,_____ And un-til we meet a-

rain fall soft up-on your fields,_____ *cresc.*

hold you, may God

-gain,_____ May God hold__ you,

30. Jesu, Lamb of God, Redeemer
(Ave verum corpus)

Medieval sequence for Corpus Christi

EDWARD ELGAR
(1857–1934)

S A (Men)
Keyboard

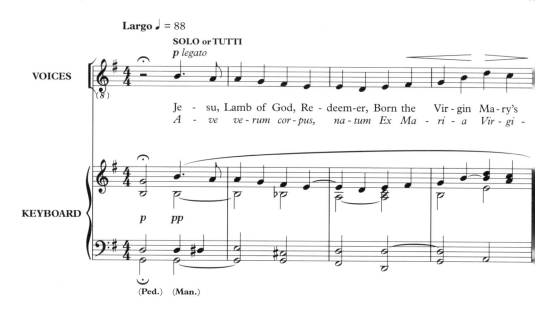

Je - su, Lamb of God, Re - deem-er, Born the Vir - gin Ma - ry's
A - ve ve - rum cor - pus, na - tum Ex Ma - ri - a Vir - gi -

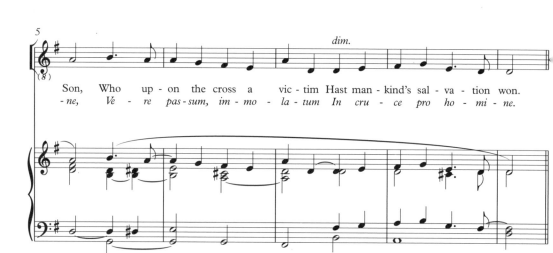

Son, Who up - on the cross a vic - tim Hast man - kind's sal - va - tion won.
- ne, Ve - re pas - sum, im - mo - la - tum In cru - ce pro ho - mi - ne.

S (A) (Men)
Keyboard

31. Jesus Christ the Apple Tree

From *Divine Hymns or Spiritual Songs*
compiled by Joshua Smith, New Hampshire, 1784

Somerset folk song
collected by Cecil Sharp
arr. ALAN BULLARD (b. 1947)

* This line may be sung an octave higher by a third upper-voice part.

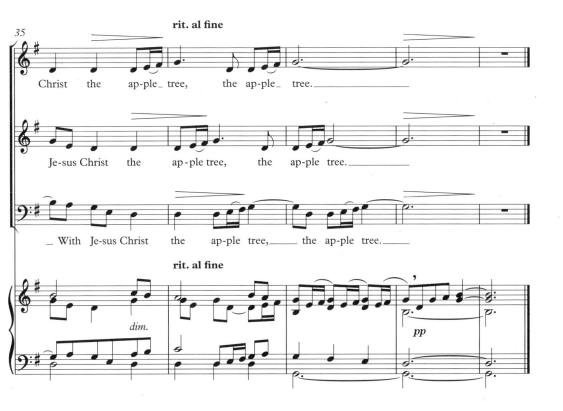

Voices 1 2 (3) (4)
(Keyboard)*

32. Jubilate
(Let us praise you)

English text by Alan Bullard

attrib. W. A. MOZART (1756–91)
arr. Alan Bullard

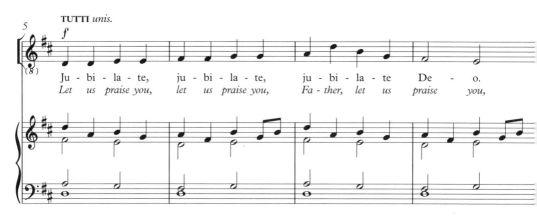

* If performing unaccompanied, begin at bar 27. The four parts may be sung by any combination of voices, including SATB.

Voices 1 (2)
Keyboard

33. Lamb of God
(Agnus Dei)

SAMUEL WEBBE
(1740–1816)

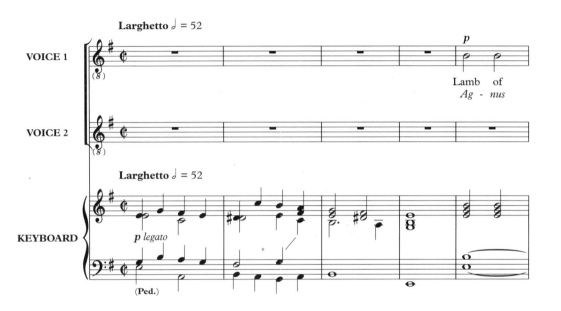

* If performing in unison, sing Voice 2 in bars 21–8.

148

Voices 1 (2)
Keyboard

34. Let all mortal flesh
keep silence

Liturgy of St James
trans. Gerard Moultrie

French caro
arr. STEPHEN CLEOBURY (b. 1948

* If voices are tutti, left-hand D should be an octave lower.

Voices 1 (2)
Keyboard

35. Like the murmur of the dove's song

Carl P. Daw
(b. 1944)

ALAN SMITH
(b. 1962)

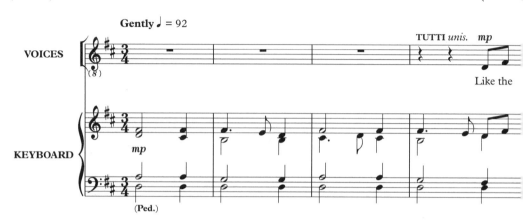

13 come, Ho - ly Spi - rit, come.

17 VOICE 1 or TUTTI
To the mem - bers of Christ's Bo - dy, to the

21 VOICE 2 or TUTTI
branch-es of the vine, to the Church in faith as - sem - bled, to her

25 TUTTI
midst as gift and sign: come, Ho - ly Spi - rit, come.

S (A) (Men)
Keyboard

36. Lord, in thy mercy

Martin Luther (1483–1546)
English version by John Rutter

FELIX MENDELSSOHN
(1809–47)

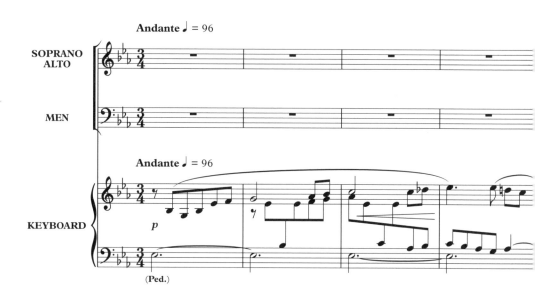

Performance suggestion: repeat bars 7–32, using solo voice the first time (upper part) and full choir in two parts the second time, as in Mendelssohn's original.

S (A) (Men)
Keyboard

37. Never
weather-beaten sail

Words and music by
THOMAS CAMPION (1567–1620)
adap. Alan Bullard

S A (T) (B)
Keyboard

38. Now the green blade rises

J. M. C. Crum
(1872–1958)

Trad. French
arr. ALAN BULLARD (b. 1947)

T./B. *unis.* **(or A.)**
p
In the grave they laid him, Love whom we had slain, Think-ing that he ne - ver

would a - wake a - gain, Laid in the earth like grain that sleeps un - seen:

(Organ: Ped. 16')

TUTTI *unis.*
(*p*) *mf*

(Organ: Ped. 8')

S./T. *f* *unis.*
A./B.
Love is come a - gain,_ like wheat that springs up green._

f

S./A. *unis.* **(or S.)** *mf*
Forth he came at Eas - ter, like the_ ri - sen grain,

T./B. *unis.* **(or A.)** *mf*
Forth he came at Eas - ter, like the_ ri - sen

mp gently and smoothly

(Man.)

S (A) (Men)
Keyboard

39. O Breath of life

Bessie Porter Head
(1850–1936)

Trad. English
arr. ALAN BULLARD (b. 1947)

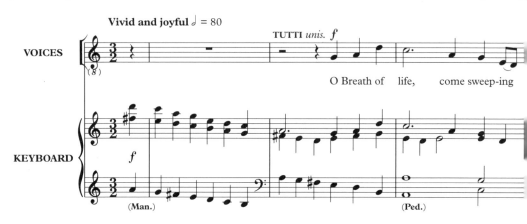

Vivid and joyful ♩ = 80

TUTTI *unis.* *f*

VOICES

O Breath of   life,   come sweep-ing

KEYBOARD

f

(Man.)   (Ped.)

4

through us,   Re - vive your church   with   life   and_ pow'r;   O Breath of

7

life,   come, cleanse, re - new us,   And fit_ your   church   to meet this   hour._____

S A (T) (B)*
Keyboard

40. O for a closer walk with God

William Cowper
(1731–1800)

CHARLES VILLIERS STANFORD
(1852–1924)

* Sing bass rather than tenor if few men are available.

(**Piano:** repeat tied bass notes as required)

(**Organ:** Ped. 8ve lower)

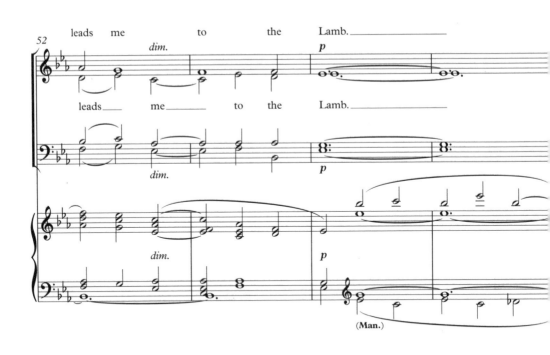

Voices 1 (2)
Keyboard

41. O God of mercy

Godfrey Thring
(1823–1903)

SIMON LOLE
(b. 1957)

42. O God, your goodness

S (A) (T) (B)
Keyboard

Christian Gellert (1715–69)
trans. Alan Bullard

L. van BEETHOVEN (1770–1827)
lower voice parts by Alan Bullard

* If performing in unison, sing the alto part from bar 26 to the end of bar 33.

43a. O praise God
in his holiness
(Version 1)

Psalm 150 (BCP)

JOHN WELDON
(1676–1736)

* An arrangement for fewer voices is provided in Version 2.

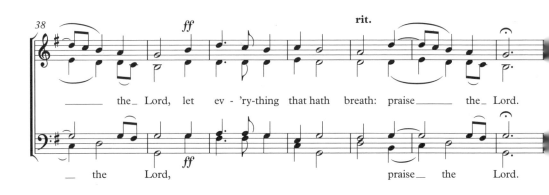

S (A) (Men)
(Keyboard)*

43b. O praise God in his holiness
(Version 2)

Psalm 150 (BCP)

JOHN WELDON
(1676–1736)

* The keyboard part (and the introduction) may be omitted if all three voice parts are sung.

Voices 1 (2)
Keyboard

44. Panis angelicus
(Bread of the angel host)

St Thomas Aquinas (1226–74)
English text by John Rutter

CÉSAR FRANCK
(1822–90)

Voices 1 (2)
Keyboard

45. Peace between nations

Trad. Hebridean (adap.)

CHRISTOPHER WIGGINS
(b. 1956)

Peace be-tween bro-thers,_____

peace____ be-tween sis - ters. Peace be-tween lo - vers in____

poco meno mosso

love of the King of Life,____ in__ love of the King of Life._____

Voices 1 (2)
Keyboard

46. Pie Jesu
(Blessed Jesu, Lord, I pray)

Anon.
trans. John Rutter

GABRIEL FAURÉ
(1845–1924)

198

47. Praise to the Trinity

Original Latin words and music by
HILDEGARD OF BINGEN (1098–1179)
edited and adapted by Julian Elloway

Unis.
(Keyboard)

The plainsong original has no performance indications. This offers much flexibility in performance, for example:

- Upper voices, optionally supported by a drone on D and A in the lower voices
- All voices in unison, optionally accompanied by a keyboard drone
- Two groups of voices, optionally accompanied by a keyboard drone, and following the bracketed suggestions: Voice 1 could be upper voices and Voice 2 could be men, or Voice 1 could be sopranos and Voice 2 altos.

The composer uses the word 'creatrix', i.e. a female creator, in the second line.

Sing with confidence and expression, thinking steady quavers, but responding freely to the shape of the phrases.

to Mrs D. R. Marlowe and the Dudden Hill Girls' School Choir

S S (A) (T) (B)
Keyboard

48. A Prayer of St Richard of Chichester

St Richard of Chichester
(*c.*1197–1253)

L. J. WHITE (b. 1910)
lower voice parts by Alan Bullard

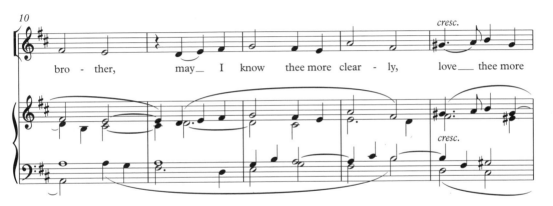

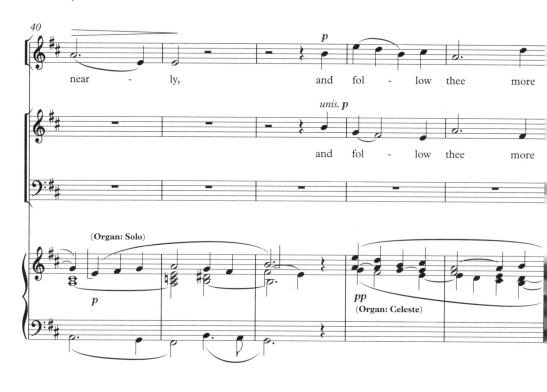

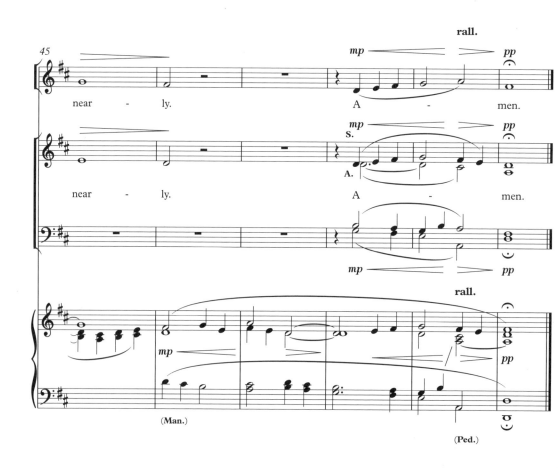

S (A) (Men)
Keyboard

49. Psalm 150

The Book of Common Prayer

BOB CHILCOTT
(b. 1955)

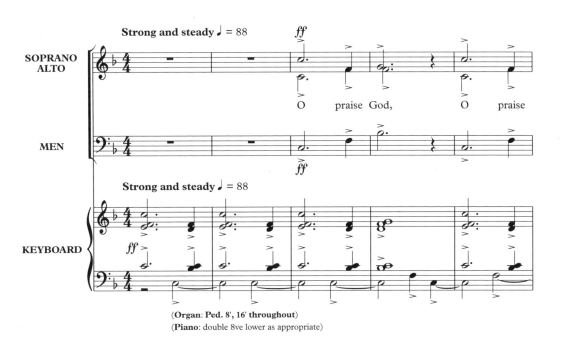

(**Organ**: Ped. 8', 16' throughout)
(**Piano**: double 8ve lower as appropriate)

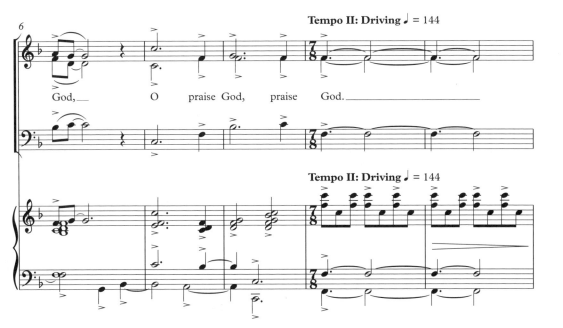

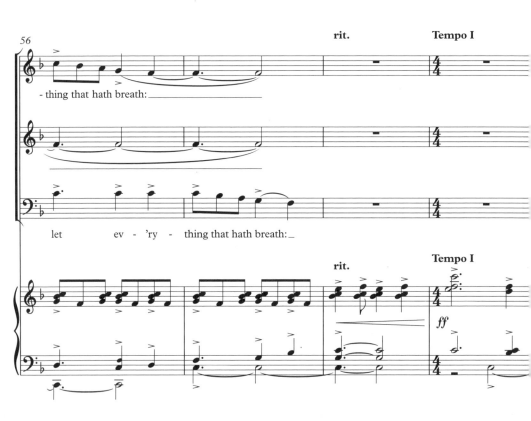

praise   the   Lord,   praise   the   Lord, ___

Tempo II

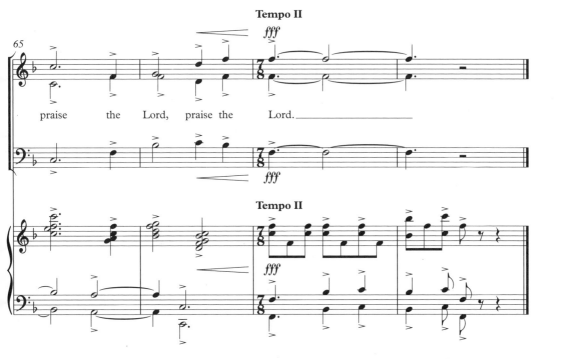

praise   the   Lord,   praise the   Lord. _____

Tempo II

Voices 1 (2)
Keyboard

50. Rejoice in the Lord alway

Philippians 4: 4–5

CHRISTOPHER WIGGIN
(b. 1956

Lord__ al - way:_____ Re - joice, re - joice, re - joice in__ the__

Lord,   and a - gain,   and a - gain   I say, re -

- joice!   I say, re - joice!

Voices 1 2 (3) (4)
(Keyboard)
(Percussion)

51. Shout for Joy!

American spiritual
arr. ALAN BULLARD (b. 194...

* Omit this stave when performing on piano or manuals only.

52. Star of Wonder

S (A) (Men)
Keyboard

John Henry Hopkins
(1820–91)

ALAN BULLARD
(b. 1947)

1. We three kings of O-ri-ent are; Bear-ing gifts we tra-verse a-far Field and foun-tain, moor and moun-tain, Fol-low-ing, fol-low-ing yon-der star:

Star of won-der, star of night, Star with roy-al beau-ty bright, West-ward lead-ing,

Guide us to thy per-fect light.

still pro-ceed-ing, Guide us to thy per-fect light.

still pro-ceed-ing, Guide us to thy per-fect light.

(Organ: opt. Solo Flute or Reeds)

THREE SOLOS or THREE GROUPS or TUTTI

mf (f) (p)

2. Born a king on Beth-le-hem plain, Gold I bring, to crown him a-gain,
3. Frank-in-cense to of-fer have I: In-cense owns a De-i-ty nigh:
4. Myrrh is mine; its bit-ter per-fume Breathes a life of gath-er-ing gloom;

King for ev-er, ceas-ing ne-ver, O-ver us, o-ver us all to reign:
Prayer and prais-ing all men rais-ing, Wor-ship him, wor-ship him, God most high:
Sor-row-ing, sigh-ing, bleed-ing, dy-ing, Sealed in the stone-cold tomb:

S (A) Men
Keyboard

53. The eternal gifts of Christ the King

Pre-11th cent.
trans. J. M. Neale

Melody: GUIDETTI (1582)
arr. Henry G. Ley (1887–1962)

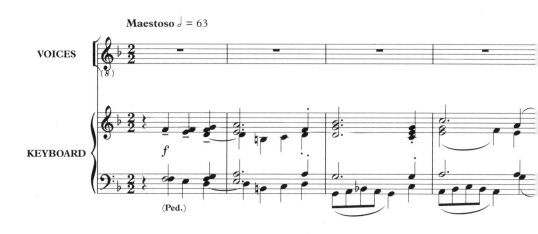

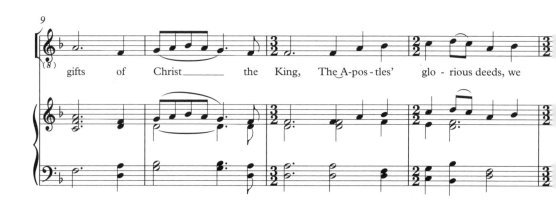

Christ that knows not   shame,_____   The   prince of this_____ world

o - ver - came.

(Ped.)

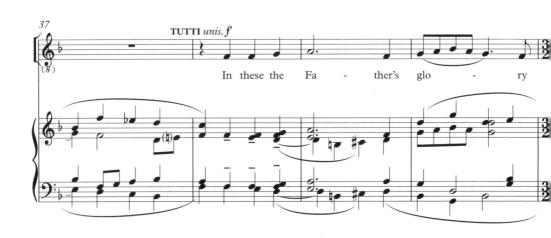

TUTTI *unis.* *f*

In these the   Fa - ther's   glo - ry

love,   That with this   glo-rious band a - bove,   Here-af-ter,   of thine end-less

grace,_____   Thy   ser-vants al - so   may__ have

may_____ have

allargando

ff

S.   place.   A - - - men.

ff

A.   place.   A - - - men.

ff

MEN   place.   A - - - men.

allargando

ff

54. The heav'ns sing praises to God

Christian Gellert (1715–69)
trans. anon.

L. van BEETHOVEN (1770–1827)
lower voice parts by Alan Bullard

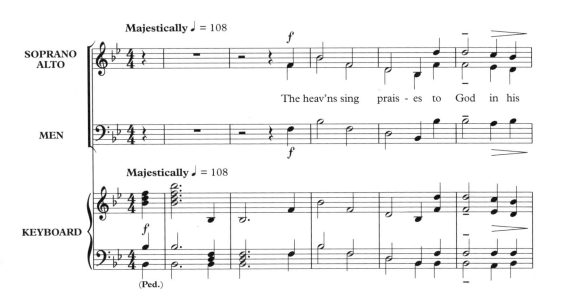

The heav'ns sing prais - es to God in his

glo - ry, And all earth ech - oes with his___ name. The un - i -

us the migh - ty sun?   That shines so   bright - ly, so

bright - ly up - on   us, And lights our path as we sing praise, and

lights our path as we sing praise!

SATB
(Keyboard)*

55a. The Lord ascendeth up on high
(Version 1)

Arthur T. Russell
(1806–74)

MICHAEL PRAETORIUS (1571–1621)
ed. Timothy Morris

Lively and joyous ♩. = 60

1. The Lord as - cend - eth up on high, The Lord hath
2. The heav'ns with joy re - ceive their Lord, By saints, by
3. Our great High Priest hath gone be - fore, Up - on his

tri - umphed glo - rious - ly, In power and might ex - cel -
an - gel hosts a - dored; O day of ex - ul - ta -
Church his grace to pour; And still his love he giv -

- ling; The grave and hell are cap - tive led. Lo! he re -
- tion! O earth, ad - ore thy glo - rious King! His ri - sing,
- eth. O may our hearts to him as - cend; May all with -

- turns, our glo - rious Head, To his e - ter - nal dwell - ing.
his as - cen - sion sing With grate - ful ad - or - a - tion.
- in us up - ward tend To him who ev - er liv - eth!

* This SATB version may be combined with the keyboard part of Version 2 on the following page by allowing four bars' rest for the introduction and between the verses, and by repeating the last four bars of the last verse.

Voices 1 2
Keyboard*

55b. The Lord ascendeth up on high
(Version 2)

Arthur T. Russell
(1806–74)

MICHAEL PRAETORIUS (1571–1621)
arr. Alan Bullard

Lively and joyous ♩. = 60

TUTTI *unis.* *f*

VOICES

KEYBOARD

mf

f (Organ: LH)

(Man.)

(Ped.)

The Lord as-cend-eth up on high, The Lord hath tri-umphed glo-rious-ly, In power and might ex-cel-ling; The grave and hell are cap-tive led. Lo!

mf

f

mf

f

mf

f

* This keyboard part may also be combined with the SATB version on the previous page.

VOICE 1 or TENOR

-tion! O_ earth, ad - ore_ thy glo - rious King! His_ ris - ing, his_ as -

VOICE 2 or BASS

(Ped.)

-cen - sion sing With grate - ful ad - or - a - tion.

VOICE 1

Our great High Priest hath gone_ be - fore, Up - on   his Church his

VOICE 2

56. The Lord bless you
and keep you

Numbers 6: 24

JOHN RUTTER
(b. 1945)

* The original version of the accompaniment, for organ, is compatible with the voice parts of this arrangement (though in G flat), and is found in the SATB version of the anthem (978–0–19–351128–6) and *John Rutter Anthems* (978–0–19–353417–9).

* If tenors are available, they may sing the alto part from here to bar 27, as well as, or instead of, altos.

peace,_____ and give you peace,_____ and give you

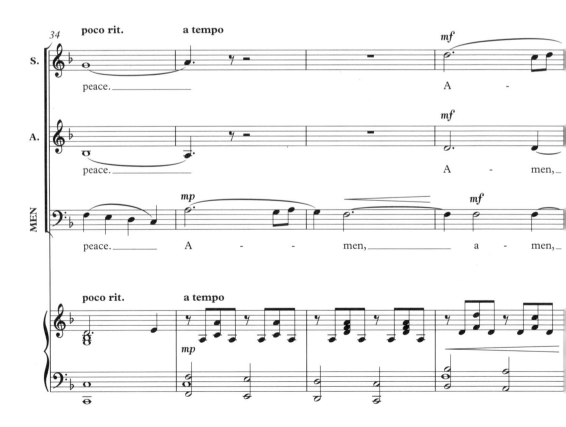

peace._____

peace._____

peace._____ A - - men,_____ a - men,_____

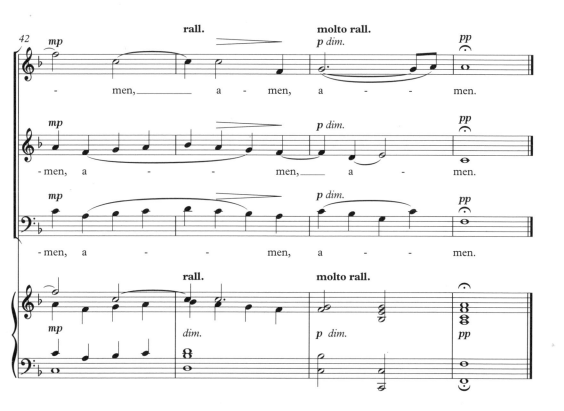

to Neil and Kristen on the occasion of their marriage, 5 May 2007

57. The Lord's my Shepherd

Psalm 23
The Scottish Psalter, 1650

BOB CHILCOTT
(b. 1955)

S (A) (Men)
Keyboard

S (A) (T) (B)
(Keyboard)*

58. The peace of God

Trad. Hebridean

ALAN BULLARD
(b. 1947)

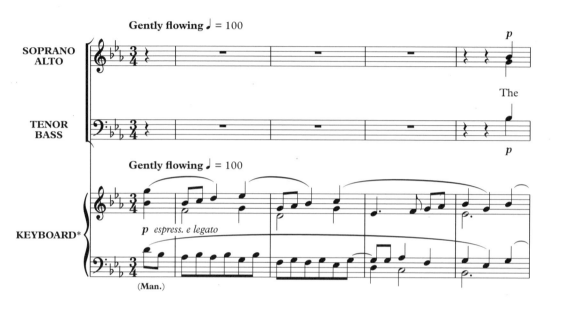

* Sing bass rather than tenor if few men are available. The keyboard part may be omitted in SATB and SAB performances.

Voices 1 (2)
Keyboard

59. There is no rose

Anon. Medieval

ANDREW SMITH
(b. 1970)

Performance suggestion: v. 1: sopranos and altos; v. 2: tenors and basses, with sopranos singing 'Res miranda' in bars 15–17; v. 3: sopranos sing the top line while altos, tenors, and basses sing the melody; v. 4: sopranos and altos, with tenors and basses joining the altos from 'Transeamus' (bar 39 to the end).

* If performing in unison, sing the lower part in bars 17–30.

* The right-hand part may be omitted in bars 32–8.

for the Music Group of St Thomas More's, Kidlington

60. The True and Living Bread

S A (Men)
Keyboard

Timothy Dudley-Smith
(b. 1926)

DAVID BLACKWELL
(b. 1961)

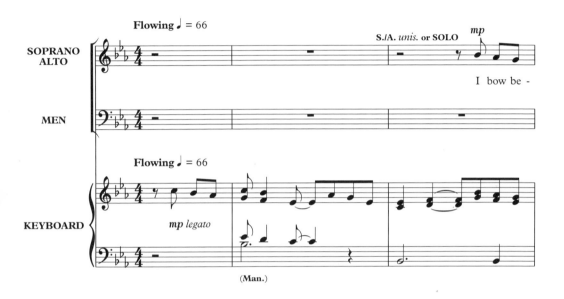

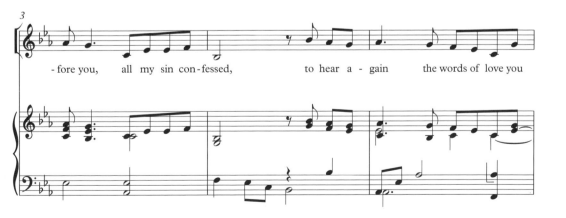

S (A) (Men)
Keyboard

61. Thou visitest the earth

Psalm 65: 9, 12

MAURICE GREENE
(1696–1755)

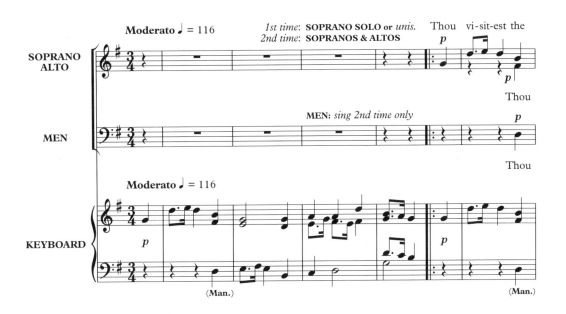

The repeat is optional. If omitting, sing tutti throughout.

S (A) (T) (B)
Keyboard

62. To be a Pilgrim

John Bunyan
(1628–88)

NICHOLAS BURT
(b. 1962)

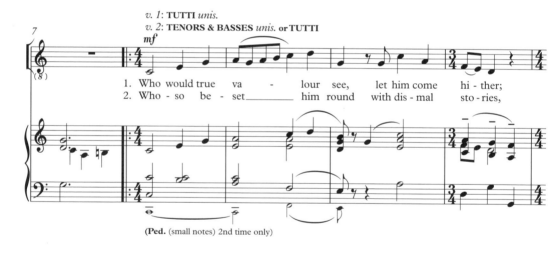

There's no dis - cou - rage-ment   shall make him   once re - lent   his first a -
No   li - on   can_ him fright,   he'll with a_   gi - ant_   fight; but he will

- vowed in - tent   to_____   be_ a   pil-grim.
have a___ right to_____   be_ a   pil-grim.

3. Hob - gob - lin   nor foul fiend can   daunt___ his   spi - rit;

he knows he at the end shall life___ in - he - rit.

Then fan - cies_ fly a-way, he'll fear not_ what men say; he'll

la - bour night and day to be_ a pil - grim.

* If performing in unison, sing the lower part in bars 46–58.

Voices 1 (2) (3)
Keyboard

63. Were you there?

American spiritual
arr. PETER HUNT (b. 1955)

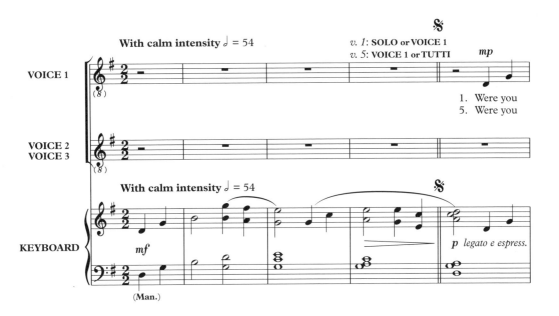

* The spiritual 'Swing low, sweet chariot' may be sung as an optional counter-melody in verse 5.

Voices 1 2
Keyboard

64. Where all charity and love are
(Ubi caritas)

11th-cent. Latin hymn for the
Exposition of the Holy Sacrament

Antiphon for Maundy Thursday
arr. ALAN BULLARD (b. 1947)

The distribution of voices between parts 1 and 2 may be varied to achieve contrasts between the phrases. The repeat for verse 2 is optional.

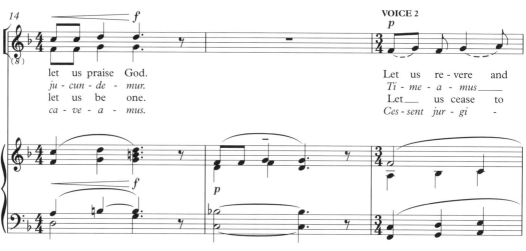

3. And with all the bless-ed com-pa - ny of saints let us see God.
3. Si - mul quo - que__ cum be - a - tis__ vi - de - a - mus.

Let us see your glo-rious and most ho-ly face: Christ the one God.
Glo-ri-an - ter__ vul-tum tu - um.__ Chri-ste De - us:

Pure and un-bound - ed joy__ be__ ours,__ Je - sus Christ,__
Gau - di - um, quod__ est im - men - sum,__ at - que pro - bum.

Our___ Lord for ev - er,___ and___ ev - er,___ Je - sus Christ.
Sae-cu-la per___ in - fi - ni - ta___ sae - cu - lo - rum.

A - men,_____ A -

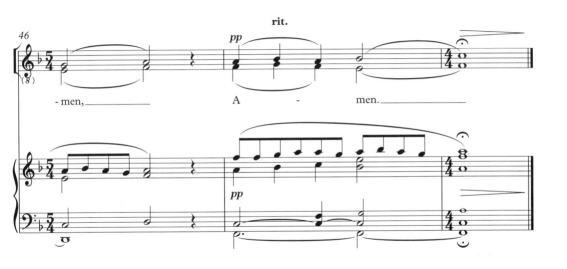

- men,_____ A - men._____

for Wendy

65. Wondrous Cross

S A (Men)
Keyboard

Isaac Watts
(1674–1748)

PHILIP WILBY
(b. 1949)

SOPRANO ALTO

Teneramente ♩ = 60

SOLO or SMALL GROUP
p espress.

When I sur-vey the won-drous cross___

MEN

KEYBOARD

Teneramente ♩ = 60

pp
(Organ: Flute/Celeste)

(Man.)

5

— On which the Prince of Glo-ry died,_____

9

My rich-est gain I count but loss,_____ And pour con -

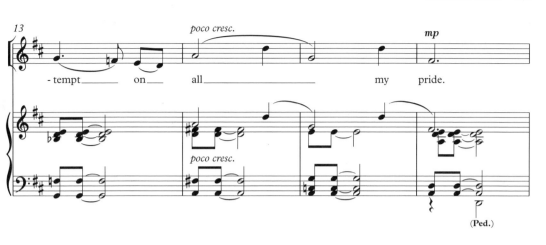

-ine, De-mands my soul, my soul, my
-ine, My soul, my
-ine, My soul, my

SOLO or SMALL GROUP

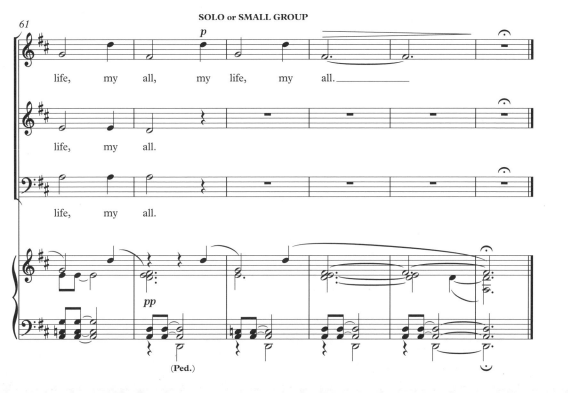

life, my all, my life, my all.
life, my all.
life, my all.

(Ped.)

Appendix: Original Versions

The practical nature of this collection means that many small editorial changes have been made without comment. This appendix lists the original (and occasionally the alternative) versions available for those anthems where more substantial alterations, additions, or arrangements have been made for the purposes of this book.

NO.	TITLE	COMPOSER	ORIGINAL VERSION(S)	AVAILABILITY
1	Alleluia	Boyce	3-part round, unaccompanied	in *Voiceworks 2*, OUP 2003
6	Christians, shout for joy and gladness	J. S. Bach	'Jesus, unser Trost und Leben', from 69 *Chorale Melodies with Figured Bass*	
7	Christ is the world's true Light	Stanton	unison with descant, organ	OUP 1943, *OEAB*
9	A Clare Benediction	Rutter	• SATB unaccompanied • SATB, organ • SSA, organ • unison/2-part, organ	OUP 1998
13	Magnificat and Nunc dimittis	Shera	• Magnificat: SATB, organ • Nunc dimittis: unison, organ	OUP 1923 OUP 1925
17	God be in my head	Armstrong Gibbs	SATB unaccompanied or SA, organ	OUP 1958, 1959
24	He is risen	Cope	2-part, organ	OUP 1937, *OEAB*
25	Hide not thou thy face	Farrant	The SATB version is the original	Also in *NCAB*
26	Holy, holy, holy, Holy is the Lord	Schubert	From *German Mass*; voice parts unaltered	
29	Irish Blessing	Chilcott	SATB, piano or SA, piano	OUP 1997
30	Jesu, Lamb of God, Redeemer	Elgar	SATB, organ	*NCAB*
32	Jubilate	Mozart	4-part round, unaccompanied	in *Voiceworks 2*, OUP 2003
36	Lord, in thy mercy	Mendelssohn	*Verleih uns Frieden*, SATB, organ (originally orchestra)	*ESM*
37	Never weather-beaten sail	Campion	From *First Book of Ayres*, solo voice and lute	
40	O for a closer walk with God	Stanford	SATB, organ	in *A Stanford Anthology*, ed. Dibble, OUP 2004

42	O God, your goodness	Beethoven	'Bitten', No. 1 from *Gellert-Lieder*, solo voice and piano; original key: E major	
43	O praise God in his holiness	Weldon	The SATB version is the original	
44	Panis angelicus	Franck	Tenor solo, cello, harp, organ; original key: A major	SATB, org. version in *ESM*
46	Pie Jesu	Fauré	From *Requiem*; treble solo and strings; original key: B♭ major	*Requiem*, ed. Rutter, OUP 1989
48	A Prayer of St Richard of Chichester	White	unison with descant, organ; original key: E♭ major	OUP 1947, *OEAB*
53	The eternal gifts of Christ the King	Guidetti, arr. Ley	SATB, organ; includes one extra verse	OUP 1951
54	The heav'ns sing praises to God	Beethoven	'Die Ehre Gottes', No. 4 from *Gellert-Lieder*, solo voice and piano; original key: C major	
55	The Lord ascendeth up on high	Praetorius	The SATB version is the original	in *Epiphany to All Saints for Choirs*, OUP 2004
56	The Lord bless you and keep you	Rutter	SATB, organ or SA, organ; original key: G♭ major	OUP 1981
61	Thou visitest the earth	Greene	SATB, organ	*NCAB*

Abbreviations are used for the following, published by Oxford University Press.

ESM *European Sacred Music*
NCAB *New Church Anthem Book*
OEAB *Oxford Easy Anthem Book*

Titles available as separate leaflets are listed as 'OUP', followed by the date of publication.